THE CASE FOR CERTIFICATION

A Guide to the Lexcura Clinical Intelligence Certification™

FOR LAW FIRMS AND REFERRAL PARTNERS

LEXCURA SUMMIT

Lexcura Clinical Intelligence Model™ · Lexcura Clinical Intelligence Certification™

THE CASE FOR CERTIFICATION

A Guide to the Lexcura Clinical Intelligence Certification™

First Edition

ISBN-13: 979-8-9972297-6-4 (Paperback)

This guide is provided as an informational overview for law firms and referral partners. It is not a substitute for the certification program and does not confer the LCCIA™ designation.

Published by Lexcura Summit.

Clinical Intelligence for Better Litigation Decisions™

Table of Contents

About This Guide

This guide is written for law firms, litigation support managers, and referral partners who work with — or are considering working with — medical-legal consultants and analysts. It is not a substitute for the Lexcura Clinical Intelligence Certification™ program itself, and it is not designed to teach the Lexcura Clinical Intelligence Model™. Analysts still need to complete the certification to earn the credential; firms still need the certification to know what they are relying on when they engage one.

What this guide does is answer the questions a hiring partner, a general counsel, or a litigation support director actually asks before extending trust to an outside analyst: What is this credential. What does it certify. Why does a structured methodology matter more in this field than in most. What separates a certified analyst from an uncertified one. And what, specifically, does a person go through to earn it.

The chapters that follow are organized in six parts. The first explains the problem the certification exists to solve — the risk inherent in medical-legal analysis performed without a consistent, defensible methodology. The second introduces the Lexcura Clinical Intelligence Model™ at the level a referring firm needs to understand it, without teaching the model's internal analytical technique. The third and fourth explain what the credential actually achieves and why it has become necessary rather than optional. The fifth walks through what the certification program entails, module by module, so a firm can understand the rigor behind the credential without needing to sit through the coursework itself. The sixth addresses the practical question every referral relationship eventually raises: how should a firm work with, evaluate, and require this credential.

Throughout, we refer to the certification's central methodology as the Lexcura Clinical Intelligence Model™, its seven components as the Seven Pillars, and its credential as the Lexcura Certified Clinical Intelligence Analyst™ designation, or LCCIA™. These are proprietary terms, and they appear capitalized and trademarked throughout this guide deliberately — they identify a specific, defined standard, not a generic description of careful record review.

PART ONE

"

A report that reads well is not the same thing as a report that will survive cross-examination.

THE LEXCURA CLINICAL INTELLIGENCE MODEL™

PART ONE

THE PROBLEM THIS CREDENTIAL SOLVES

Why trust alone is no longer enough when retaining a medical-legal analyst.

Chapter 1 — The Trust Problem in Medical-Legal Consulting

Every litigation support director eventually confronts the same quiet problem. A case arrives with thousands of pages of medical records. An analyst or consultant is retained to review them. Weeks later, a report comes back — organized, confident, and seemingly thorough. But the attorney reading it has no reliable way to know whether that confidence is earned.

This is not a criticism of the consultants who do this work. It is a structural problem in a field that, for decades, has had no consistent standard for what "medical record review" actually requires. Two analysts can review the identical set of records and produce meaningfully different conclusions — not because one is dishonest, but because the field itself has never agreed on a repeatable method for turning medical documentation into legal intelligence. One analyst may focus heavily on the discharge summary and the final diagnosis. Another may work chronologically through nursing notes. A third may center the entire review around the moment an adverse outcome occurred, reasoning backward from there. All three might be diligent. All three might reach different conclusions on the same case.

For a firm relying on that work product, this variability is a liability that is easy to underestimate. A report that reads well is not the same thing as a report that will survive cross-examination. An analysis that "feels" thorough is not the same thing as an analysis built on a defensible, repeatable methodology that can be explained, defended, and, if necessary, taught to a jury. The gap between those two things rarely becomes visible until a deposition, a Daubert challenge, or an opposing expert exposes it — at which point it is the firm's case, not the consultant's reputation, that absorbs the cost.

The trust problem, stated plainly, is this: hiring a medical-legal analyst has historically required taking their competence on faith. A resume, a list of past cases, a confident writing style — none of these reliably indicate whether the person applies a consistent analytical framework or simply produces a well-organized narrative of what they happened to notice. There has been no external, verifiable standard a firm could point to and say, with confidence, "this person's methodology has been tested and validated."

That is the gap the Lexcura Clinical Intelligence Certification™ was built to close. It does not simply ask whether an analyst can write a competent-sounding summary of a medical record. It tests whether that analyst can consistently apply a specific, structured, seven-part methodology — the same methodology, applied the same way, on every case, by every certified analyst who holds the credential. The chapters that follow explain what that methodology is, what the certification actually verifies, and why that verification has become something firms increasingly cannot afford to do without.

Chapter 2 — Information Is Not Intelligence

The Lexcura Clinical Intelligence Model™ begins from a distinction that sounds simple and turns out to be the single most important idea in the entire methodology: information is not the same thing as intelligence.

A medical record, however large, is a collection of information. A vital sign reading is information. A physician's note is information. A laboratory value, a medication administration record, an imaging report — each is a discrete fact, generated at a moment in time, and each is, by itself, largely inert. It documents something. It does not, on its own, explain anything.

Intelligence is what emerges when that information is organized, connected, and interpreted — when a reviewer asks not "what was recorded here" but "what does this mean, in relation to everything else in this case." A single elevated lactate value is a data point. That same value, understood against a patient's baseline, placed on a timeline alongside a delayed physician response and a subsequent rapid deterioration, becomes something else entirely: evidence of a preventable harm, or evidence that harm was unavoidable, depending on what the fuller picture shows.

This distinction matters because it explains why thorough documentation review so often fails to produce a useful legal work product. A reviewer can read every page of a ten-thousand-page chart, accurately summarize what each page says, and still fail to answer the only questions that matter to the case: what happened, why it happened, whether it should have happened, and whether it changed the outcome. Comprehensive is not the same as intelligent. A case summary can be exhaustive and still miss the finding that would have changed the outcome of the litigation.

The Lexcura Clinical Intelligence Model™ exists to close that gap deliberately. Rather than leaving the transition from information to intelligence to an individual analyst's instinct or experience, it structures that transition into a defined sequence of analytical steps — the Seven Pillars, introduced in Part Two of this guide — each of which asks a specific question the evidence must answer before the analysis can move forward. The result, when the methodology is applied correctly, is not simply a summary of what the records say. It is an explanation of what the records mean, built in a sequence that can be shown, defended, and reproduced.

This is also why certification, rather than experience alone, has become the meaningful credential in this space. Experience teaches an analyst to notice things. It does not, by itself, teach a repeatable method for converting what is noticed into a structured, defensible finding. That is a skill that has to be taught deliberately and tested directly — which is exactly what the certification program is designed to do.

There is one further point firms often underestimate here: an experienced but uncertified analyst can absolutely notice the right things on any given case. The risk is not that experience fails every time. The risk is that it fails inconsistently, in ways that are invisible until they are tested — and litigation is, almost by definition, the process of testing an analysis that was not built to withstand scrutiny. A structured methodology does not replace an analyst's clinical or investigative judgment. It gives that judgment a consistent scaffold, so that the analyst's experience is applied the same disciplined way on every case, rather than being left to reconstruct the right sequence of questions from instinct alone, under time pressure, on each new matter.

Chapter 3 — Why Traditional Record Review Falls Short

Traditional medical record review, as it has typically been practiced in litigation support, tends to organize itself around a chronology or a summary — a narrative account of what the records contain, arranged roughly in the order events occurred. This approach is not without value. It gives an attorney a readable account of the case. But it has three structural weaknesses that surface as soon as a case is contested.

The first is that a chronological summary tends to document the obvious and understate the subtle. Major events — a code, a transfer to a higher level of care, a documented complication — are easy to find and easy to describe. The findings that most often decide close cases are rarely the obvious ones. They are the gradual laboratory trend that crossed a meaningful threshold three shifts before anyone charted a concern about it. The vital sign pattern that, in isolation, looked unremarkable, but in the context of the patient's baseline was a clear early warning. A narrative summary, built around what was documented as significant at the time, has no structural mechanism for surfacing what nobody flagged as significant in the moment.

The second weakness is that traditional review rarely separates the evaluation of the record's own reliability from the evaluation of its contents. Before any conclusion can be drawn from a medical record, a reviewer has to know how much confidence that record actually deserves — whether documentation is complete, internally consistent, and free of the kind of contradictions and gaps that would undermine reliance on it. A review that moves directly into summarizing the narrative, without first assessing whether the narrative can be trusted, risks building a sophisticated analysis on an unstable foundation.

The third weakness is perhaps the most consequential for litigation specifically: traditional review often conflates "what happened" with "what should have happened" with "whether it mattered." These are three separate analytical questions, and answering them in sequence, with discipline, is what allows a finding to hold up under cross-examination. A report that blends outcome, standard of care, and causation into a single narrative impression is vulnerable the moment an opposing expert asks the reviewer to separate those threads — because the reviewer, without a structured method requiring that separation from the outset, may not have actually done so.

None of this means traditional reviewers are careless. It means the traditional approach to record review was never built as a structured methodology in the first place — it evolved as a practice, refined by individual habit and experience, without an agreed external standard. The Lexcura Clinical Intelligence Model™ was designed specifically to correct these three weaknesses: it assesses record reliability first, before any substantive conclusion is drawn; it uses a structured baseline-to-outcome framework designed to surface subtle findings rather than only obvious ones; and it separates the analytical questions of fact, standard, and causation into distinct, sequential pillars, so that each conclusion can be defended on its own terms. What that framework actually contains is the subject of Part Two.

It is also worth noting that these three weaknesses tend to compound rather than occur in isolation. A review that has not first assessed record reliability is more likely to miss subtle findings, because a reviewer who has not identified gaps or contradictions in the documentation has no way of knowing which parts of the record deserve the closest scrutiny. A review that misses subtle findings is, in turn, more likely to collapse fact, standard, and causation into a single narrative impression, simply because there is less material available to support a more granular analysis. Correcting any one weakness in isolation would help. Correcting all three, in a fixed sequence that prevents each from reinforcing the others, is what a genuine methodology — rather than a set of good individual habits — actually provides.

Chapter 4 — A Composite Case, Viewed Two Ways

Abstract arguments about methodology are easier to evaluate against a concrete example, so consider a composite case — not drawn from any single matter, but representative of the pattern that recurs across medical-legal litigation involving a delayed diagnosis and a disputed standard of care.

A patient is admitted for a scheduled procedure with an unremarkable medical history. Over the following thirty-six hours, a series of small changes appear across the record: a laboratory value drifts upward across several draws, a vital sign trend shows a gradual but consistent shift, and a nursing note here and there mentions the patient "not looking quite right" without further elaboration. No single entry, read on its own, describes an emergency. A rapid response is eventually called, the patient is transferred to a higher level of care, and a significant complication is later confirmed. The family retains counsel. The defense retains its own experts. Both sides need a medical-legal analyst to make sense of what the chart actually shows.

Reviewed the traditional way, this chart tends to produce one of two familiar reports. The first is a chronological narrative: it describes, in order, what happened, culminating in the rapid response and the complication, and it may note in passing that "some lab values were elevated" and that "the patient's condition changed over time." It reads competently. It does not, however, make clear whether those elevated values crossed a threshold that should have prompted earlier intervention, because it never established what a normal trend looked like for this specific patient in the first place, and it never systematically compared the objective data against the timeline to identify exactly when a reasonable provider should have recognized a problem. The second familiar report works backward from the known outcome: because the complication was serious, the reviewer treats the entire prior thirty-six hours as an unbroken chain of missed warning signs — an analysis shaped by hindsight, vulnerable to the very first question a competent cross-examiner will ask: would this have looked like a clear warning sign at the time, without knowing how it turned out?

Applied through the Lexcura Clinical Intelligence Model™, the same chart is approached differently, in a specific order. Record Integrity™ first establishes whether the documentation across nursing, laboratory, and physician sources is complete and internally consistent enough to support reliable analysis — surfacing, for instance, whether a gap in charting during a shift change obscures part of the relevant window. Baseline Profiling™ establishes what was actually normal for this patient specifically, so that the later laboratory trend can be judged against this patient's own baseline rather than a generic reference range. Imaging Analysis™ examines the objective data directly — the laboratory trend and any monitoring strips — independent of how any single note characterized it, often revealing a trajectory that becomes obviously significant only when the individual values are plotted against each other in sequence rather than read one draw at a time. Timeline Reconstruction™ then places that objective trend, the vague nursing observations, and the eventual rapid response onto a single, honest chronology, which is frequently the first point at which the gap between when the data turned and when anyone acted becomes visible at all. Only then does Standard of Care Review™ ask what a reasonable provider should have done at each point on that timeline, using only what was knowable at that moment — and only after that does Causation Mapping™ ask whether the interval between the objective warning and the eventual response actually changed the outcome, as opposed to the complication being unavoidable regardless of timing.

The point of this composite example is not that the Lexcura methodology always produces a conclusion favorable to one side or the other. Sometimes a rigorous baseline-to-outcome analysis confirms that a complication was unforeseeable and unavoidable, protecting a defendant provider from an unfair hindsight judgment; sometimes it confirms a preventable delay. The point is narrower and, for a referring firm, more important: the sequence itself is what makes the conclusion — whichever way it comes out — defensible under scrutiny, because it can be shown, step by step, that the analysis did not skip a question or answer it out of order.

PART TWO

“

Information is not intelligence. Intelligence is what emerges when evidence is organized, connected, and interpreted.

THE LEXCURA CLINICAL INTELLIGENCE MODEL™

PART TWO

THE LEXCURA CLINICAL INTELLIGENCE MODEL™

A structured, seven-part methodology for turning records into litigation-ready findings.

Chapter 5 — The Model: An Overview

The Seven Pillars, In Sequence

The Lexcura Clinical Intelligence Model™ is a structured, seven-part methodology for converting medical documentation into litigation-ready analysis. It was built on a simple premise: the order in which a case is analyzed is not incidental to the quality of the conclusion — it is central to it. Each of the Seven Pillars answers one specific question, and each pillar depends on the ones before it having been done properly. Skipping a pillar, or performing them out of sequence, does not simply produce a less thorough analysis. It produces conclusions that rest on an incomplete foundation, whether or not that incompleteness is visible in the final report.

At a level appropriate for a firm evaluating the credential — rather than an analyst learning to apply it — the Seven Pillars can be summarized as the seven questions every properly analyzed medical-legal case must answer, in this order:

Record Integrity™ asks: can the record be trusted? Before any conclusion is drawn from a medical record, the record itself must be evaluated for completeness, internal consistency, and reliability. This pillar identifies missing documentation, contradictions, and gaps that would undermine confidence in what follows.

Baseline Profiling™ asks: who was the patient before the event? Establishing a patient's pre-event condition, risk factors, and functional status is what allows a later causation analysis to distinguish between harm caused by an event and outcomes that were already in motion before it.

Imaging Analysis™ asks: has the objective evidence been examined directly? This pillar looks past narrative conclusions and summaries to the underlying objective data itself — imaging studies, laboratory trends, continuous monitoring data — on the reasoning that objective evidence often reveals a deterioration before the written narrative catches up to it.

Timeline Reconstruction™ asks: what happened, and when? This pillar organizes fragmented documentation, scattered across dozens of sources, into a coherent chronology capable of revealing delays, missed opportunities, and escalation failures that are invisible when records are read source by source rather than in sequence.

Standard of Care Review™ asks: what should have happened? Once the actual sequence of events is established, this pillar compares it against the standard of care that reasonably applied under the circumstances — deliberately not an outcome-based or hindsight judgment, but an assessment of what a reasonable provider would have done at each decision point, knowing only what was known at the time.

Regulatory & Compliance Overlay™ asks: what system duties applied? Beyond the conduct of individual providers, this pillar considers the policies, regulations, accreditation standards, and institutional obligations that governed the care setting, recognizing that some failures are systemic rather than individual.

Causation Mapping™ asks the question the entire methodology has been building toward: did any of it actually change the outcome? Identifying a delay, a variance, or a missed standard does not, by itself, establish that the delay or variance caused harm. This final analytical pillar is where the preceding six pillars are drawn together to determine whether — and how — the identified issues affected what ultimately happened to the patient.

An eighth stage, Litigation-Ready Output™, is not an analytical pillar in the same sense as the seven above; it is the discipline of translating the completed analysis into a form attorneys can immediately use — organized, prioritized, and communicated in a way that supports legal strategy rather than simply documenting clinical findings.

Litigation-Ready Output™ is treated as a distinct discipline, not an afterthought tacked onto the end of the analysis, for a specific reason. A technically excellent seven-pillar analysis that is communicated poorly — buried in clinical jargon, organized chronologically rather than by legal significance, or silent on which findings matter most to the case theory — fails the retaining attorney just as surely as a flawed analysis would. Litigation-Ready Output™ requires the analyst to make a further set of judgments: which findings are strategically significant, how they should be prioritized, and how they should be framed so that an attorney who has not spent weeks in the record can immediately grasp what matters and why. This is a communication skill as much as an analytical one, and it is treated in the certification program with the same seriousness as any of the Seven Pillars themselves.

This overview is deliberately conceptual. It tells a referring firm what each pillar is for and why it exists in the sequence it does. It does not teach the analytical techniques, evaluative criteria, or case-based methodology an analyst actually applies within each pillar — that instruction, along with the extensive practice, testing, and evaluation that goes with it, is the content of the certification program itself, and it is the reason the credential, rather than a summary of the model, is what a firm should actually be looking for when it evaluates an analyst.

A useful way to hold these seven questions in mind is to notice that each one closes off a specific way an analysis can go wrong. Record Integrity™ closes off the risk of building conclusions on unreliable evidence. Baseline Profiling™ closes off the risk of judging an outcome without knowing what was normal for this patient. Imaging Analysis™ closes off the risk of accepting a narrative summary in place of the underlying objective data. Timeline Reconstruction™ closes off the risk of missing a delay or a pattern that only becomes visible in sequence. Standard of Care Review™ closes off the risk of hindsight bias. Regulatory & Compliance Overlay™ closes off the risk of overlooking systemic, rather than individual, failure. And Causation Mapping™ closes off the risk of mistaking a documented problem for a proven cause. Seen this way, the Seven Pillars are less a checklist than a sequence of safeguards, each addressing a specific, well-documented failure mode in medical-legal analysis.

Chapter 6 — Why Sequence Is the Discipline

It would be reasonable to ask why seven analytical questions need to be asked in a fixed order rather than addressed however an experienced analyst sees fit. The answer is that each pillar in the Lexcura Clinical Intelligence Model™ produces a finding the next pillar depends on, and reversing that dependency quietly undermines the reliability of everything downstream.

Consider what happens when causation is assessed before a timeline has been properly reconstructed. An analyst working backward from a known bad outcome, without first establishing an objective chronology, is exposed to a well-documented cognitive risk: hindsight bias. Once you know how a case ended, it becomes very easy to see every prior decision as the moment that sealed that outcome, whether or not the evidence actually supports that conclusion. Building the timeline first, independent of the causation question, is what protects the analysis from being shaped by its own conclusion.

Consider, similarly, what happens when a standard-of-care judgment is formed before a patient's baseline has been established. A clinical decision that looks conservative or even negligent in isolation may be entirely reasonable once a reviewer understands what the treating providers actually knew about this specific patient's risk profile at the time. Skipping baseline analysis does not just leave out a data point — it removes the context that determines whether a later judgment about provider conduct is even fair.

This is why the certification does not simply test whether an analyst knows what each pillar is. It tests whether the analyst can apply all seven, in the correct sequence, consistently, across varied case fact patterns — including the applied case simulation and the Capstone Case Review™ described in Part Five of this guide. A firm relying on a certified analyst is relying on more than familiarity with seven concepts. It is relying on demonstrated, tested discipline in applying them in the order that keeps each conclusion honest.

It is also worth stating plainly what this model is not. It is not a checklist that can be applied mechanically without judgment, and it is not a substitute for clinical or legal expertise. It is a discipline for organizing that expertise so that it produces a consistent, defensible result regardless of which analyst applies it, on which case, on which day. That consistency is exactly what a firm needs when building a case record it may eventually have to defend in front of a jury.

This last point deserves emphasis because it addresses a fair objection to any structured methodology: doesn't standardization risk flattening the judgment and expertise that makes a good analyst valuable in the first place? The Lexcura Clinical Intelligence Model™ answers that concern by design. The model does not tell an analyst what conclusion to reach — it tells the analyst what order to ask the questions in, and what each question requires before moving to the next. Clinical judgment, investigative instinct, and case-specific expertise remain fully engaged within each pillar. What the sequence removes is not judgment; it is the risk that judgment gets applied inconsistently, out of order, or shaped by a conclusion it has not yet earned.

PART THREE

"

Certification confirms competency in the methodology. It does not confirm the outcome of any case.

THE LEXCURA CLINICAL INTELLIGENCE MODEL™

PART THREE

WHAT CERTIFICATION ACHIEVES

What the LCCIA™ credential actually certifies, and what it does not.

Chapter 7 — What the LCCIA™ Credential Certifies

The Lexcura Certified Clinical Intelligence Analyst™ designation — LCCIA™ — is awarded to individuals who have completed the full certification program and demonstrated competency in applying the Lexcura Clinical Intelligence Model™. The credential is answering a narrower, more specific question than "is this person good at reviewing medical records," and that precision matters.

The certification confirms three things. First, that the holder has been directly taught the complete Lexcura Clinical Intelligence Model™ — all Seven Pillars, in the sequence and interdependency described in Part Two — rather than having absorbed a general familiarity with medical-legal analysis through unstructured experience. Second, that the holder has demonstrated the ability to apply each pillar individually, tested through module-specific knowledge checks and scored quizzes across the certification curriculum. Third, and most importantly, that the holder has demonstrated the ability to apply all seven pillars together, in an integrated fashion, against realistic case material — tested through an applied case simulation, a fully evaluated Capstone Case Review™, and a comprehensive Final Certification Examination™ covering the complete methodology.

What the credential does not certify is equally important, and Lexcura is deliberate about this distinction. Certification validates competency in the methodology. It is not, by itself, an authorization to practice as an analyst on live litigation matters, and it does not encompass the professional governance, attorney-communication standards, report-production requirements, or operational procedures that surround real-world engagement. Those elements are addressed through a separate credential — the Licensed Use Authorization™ Program — discussed further in Chapter 16. This separation exists for the same reason a firm would not want it any other way: it keeps the certification focused on a single, testable question — does this person know and can they apply the methodology — rather than blending competency with a broader set of professional and operational requirements that are better evaluated separately.

For a referring firm, this means the LCCIA™ credential should be read as a specific, verifiable claim: this analyst has been taught a defined methodology and has been tested — not merely asked, but tested, across knowledge checks, quizzes, a case simulation, a capstone case review, and a comprehensive final examination — on their ability to apply it. That is a meaningfully different, and meaningfully more reliable, signal than years of experience or a well-written writing sample.

The limits of that claim deserve the same directness. Certification is a statement about methodology, not a guarantee about outcome, workload capacity, subject-matter specialization within medicine, or fit for a particular case. A firm should still ask the ordinary due-diligence questions it would ask of any consultant. What certification changes is the starting point for that diligence: rather than beginning from zero on the question of methodology, a firm can begin from a verified baseline and spend its diligence effort on the questions certification does not answer — availability, specialization, communication style, and cost — rather than re-litigating whether the analyst's underlying process can be trusted at all.

Chapter 8 — Certification and Licensure: An Important Distinction

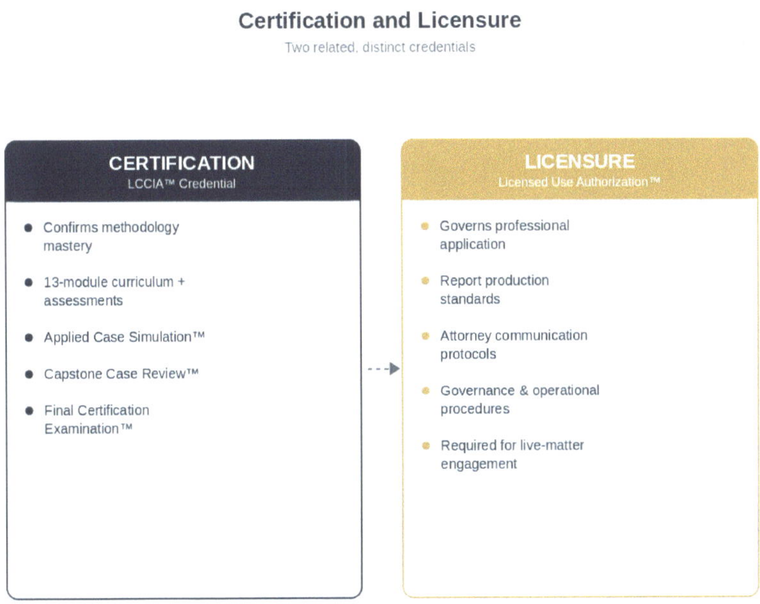

Firms new to the Lexcura credentialing structure sometimes assume that certification alone means an analyst is fully authorized and equipped to be retained for litigation work. That assumption is worth correcting directly, since understanding the distinction between certification and licensure is part of using the credential correctly.

Certification is an educational and competency credential. It confirms that the individual has completed a structured curriculum covering the Lexcura Clinical Intelligence Model™ and has passed the assessments built into that curriculum, culminating in the Final Certification Examination™. It answers the question: does this person understand and can they apply the methodology.

Licensure — addressed through the separate Licensed Use Authorization™ Program — governs professional application: how the methodology is used in actual engagements, how findings are governed and documented for professional use, how communication with retaining attorneys is structured, and what operational and governance standards apply when the methodology is put into practice on a real case. It answers a different question: is this person, and their engagement, operating under the professional standards Lexcura requires for real-world use of the model.

The reason this distinction matters to a referring firm is practical. When evaluating an analyst or a consulting relationship, a firm should ask which credential — or which combination of credentials — actually applies to the engagement being contracted for. An LCCIA™ credential tells a firm that the analyst has mastered the underlying methodology. Firms building vendor requirements or internal standards around Lexcura-trained analysts should treat certification as the baseline competency floor, and should confirm separately whether a given engagement also requires or includes the professional authorization addressed by the licensing pathway.

This two-tier structure — competency first, professional authorization second — is itself a signal of how seriously the methodology is administered. A credentialing system that collapsed education and professional authorization into a single undifferentiated designation would tell a firm less, not more, about what it was actually relying on.

A helpful analogy, though an imperfect one, is the distinction familiar from other professional fields between completing a course of training and holding a license to practice independently. A firm would not assume that completing a training curriculum, by itself, authorizes someone to operate without further oversight in a professional context that carries its own governance requirements. The Lexcura structure applies that same logic deliberately: certification confirms the training and testing have been completed to a rigorous standard; licensure addresses the separate question of professional operation. Firms that internalize this distinction are better equipped to ask precise questions when structuring engagements, rather than assuming a single credential answers every relevant question at once.

Chapter 9 — The Case for Working with Certified Analysts

Put simply, the case for engaging a Lexcura-certified analyst rests on the difference between hoping an analyst has a sound methodology and knowing they have been tested on one.

An uncertified analyst, however experienced, is an unknown quantity with respect to methodology specifically. They may be excellent. They may apply something functionally similar to the Lexcura model through years of hard-won instinct. Or they may have significant, invisible gaps — a tendency to skip baseline analysis, a habit of reasoning backward from outcome to causation, an inconsistent approach to assessing record reliability before drawing conclusions from the record. A firm has no external, verifiable way to know which of these is true before the report lands on their desk, and often not even then.

A certified analyst has demonstrated, through a structured and independently assessed curriculum, that they apply all Seven Pillars, in sequence, to case material they did not construct themselves. That does not guarantee a perfect analysis on every case — no credential can promise that — but it substantially narrows the range of ways an analysis can go wrong. It means the record's reliability was checked before conclusions were drawn from it. It means the patient's baseline was established before causation was assessed. It means the standard-of-care judgment was formed independent of hindsight bias about the outcome. These are not incidental improvements. They are exactly the failure modes that turn a strong-seeming report into a vulnerable one under cross-examination.

There is also a reputational dimension. A firm's litigation support choices are, ultimately, part of the firm's own credibility. Retaining an analyst whose methodology cannot be independently verified is a quiet risk the firm carries into every deposition and every trial built on that analyst's work. Retaining a certified analyst allows the firm to point to an external, structured standard — one the analyst did not design and cannot self-certify — as part of the foundation for the analysis the firm is relying on.

This distinction — an external standard the analyst did not design and cannot self-certify — is worth underscoring, because it is what separates genuine credentialing from marketing language. Any analyst can describe their own process as rigorous, structured, and defensible; those are claims, not verification. A credential administered by an outside body, built around assessments the analyst does not control and cannot adjust to fit their own habits, is a different category of assurance entirely. It is the difference between a consultant telling a firm they are thorough and a firm having an independent basis to confirm it.

PART FOUR

“

Inconsistent analysis is a risk a firm carries quietly, until the moment it becomes the case's weakest point.

THE LEXCURA CLINICAL INTELLIGENCE MODEL™

PART FOUR

WHY CERTIFICATION IS NECESSARY

The risk, cost, and reputational case for requiring a verified standard.

Chapter 10 — The Cost of Inconsistent Analysis

It helps to be direct about what is actually at stake when medical-legal analysis is inconsistent. The cost does not show up as a line item. It shows up later, and it shows up in the moments that matter most: a deposition where an analyst cannot clearly explain why they reached a conclusion in the order they reached it; a Daubert or Frye challenge that targets the absence of a defined, repeatable methodology; a cross-examination that exposes a causation opinion built without a properly established baseline or timeline.

Inconsistent analysis is also expensive in a quieter way. A firm that cannot rely on a consistent methodology across its consulting relationships is, in effect, re-litigating the reliability question on every single case. Every new analyst is a new unknown. Every report requires the retaining attorney to independently sanity-check the analytical approach, because there is no shared standard guaranteeing that this analyst approached the case the same way the last one did. That is time and risk a firm should not have to carry on every engagement.

Certification exists to convert that recurring, case-by-case uncertainty into a one-time verification. Once a firm understands what the LCCIA™ credential certifies, it does not need to re-evaluate methodology from scratch every time it retains a certified analyst — it can trust that the same Seven Pillars, applied in the same sequence, are being applied here as they were on the last engagement, because the credential itself is the evidence of that consistency.

This is, in effect, an efficiency argument as much as a quality argument. Every hour a litigation support team spends independently vetting an analyst's approach on a new matter is an hour not spent on case strategy, and every re-evaluation carries its own risk of error, since the person doing the vetting is rarely a specialist in medical-legal methodology themselves. Certification does not eliminate the need for oversight of the work product on any individual case — a firm should still review what it receives — but it substantially reduces the burden of verifying, from scratch, whether the underlying process can be trusted in the first place.

Chapter 11 — Standardization and Cross-Examination Readiness

A medical-legal analysis is not truly finished until it has been imagined under cross-examination. An opposing expert or attorney will look for exactly the vulnerabilities that inconsistent methodology creates: Did you consider the patient's baseline before reaching your causation opinion, or after? Can you walk me through how you assessed the reliability of this record before relying on it? Did you form your standard-of-care opinion independent of knowing how the case turned out, or with that knowledge already in hand?

An analyst applying the Lexcura Clinical Intelligence Model™ has a structural answer to each of these questions, because the methodology requires answering them in a specific, defensible order as a condition of the analysis being complete at all. Record Integrity™ is assessed first so that the analyst can testify that record reliability was evaluated before, not after, substantive conclusions were drawn. Baseline Profiling™ precedes Causation Mapping™ so the analyst can testify that the patient's pre-event condition was established independent of the outcome. And Standard of Care Review™ is structured to evaluate what a reasonable provider knew at each decision point, so the analyst can testify that hindsight was never allowed to substitute for a contemporaneous standard.

Here is what standardization actually buys a litigating firm: not a guarantee of a favorable outcome, but a process that holds together under pressure and can be walked through, in plain terms, in front of a jury, because it was built from the outset to answer the challenges a rigorous cross-examination will raise. A firm evaluating whether to require certification of its consulting relationships should weigh this specifically — not whether the analyst seems capable, but whether the analyst's process will hold up when someone with every incentive to find its weak point goes looking for one.

There is a further, quieter benefit to standardization that surfaces well before any cross-examination: internal case preparation itself becomes easier. When an attorney knows that an analysis was built pillar by pillar, in a fixed sequence, preparing that analyst for deposition or trial testimony becomes a matter of walking through a known structure rather than reverse-engineering an idiosyncratic process after the fact. The same structure that protects the analysis under adversarial scrutiny also makes it easier for the retaining attorney to understand, question, and ultimately present it.

Chapter 12 — Protecting Firm Reputation and Referral Relationships

Referral relationships in the litigation support and expert consulting space run in both directions. A firm refers business to consultants it trusts; consultants and referral partners, in turn, are often judged by the quality of the analysts and experts they recommend. A firm that builds a reputation for retaining rigorously credentialed analysts is protecting more than any single case — it is protecting the referral relationships and professional reputation that generate future business.

Requiring, or at minimum preferring, Lexcura certification as part of a firm's vendor standards accomplishes something a firm cannot easily accomplish case by case: it creates a consistent, defensible standard the firm can point to across its entire book of medical-legal litigation, not just the cases where a particularly diligent partner happened to vet the analyst carefully. It also gives litigation support directors and hiring partners a clear, non-arbitrary basis for a decision that might otherwise be difficult to defend internally — "we require this credential" is a more durable policy than "we liked this consultant's prior work."

There is a downstream benefit as well. As more firms come to recognize and specifically request the LCCIA™ credential, holding it becomes a meaningful differentiator for analysts and a meaningful risk-reduction signal for the firms that retain them — a virtuous cycle that raises the floor for the entire field, rather than leaving quality assessment to each firm's individual diligence, repeated case after case, indefinitely.

None of this requires a firm to treat certification as the only consideration in a hiring decision. Reputation, specialization, and track record still matter, and should. The point is narrower: certification gives a firm a verifiable floor beneath those other considerations, so that reputation and track record are being evaluated on top of a confirmed methodological standard, rather than substituting for one.

Chapter 13 — Risk Management, Insurance, and the Necessity Argument

There is a version of the argument for certification that has nothing to do with quality of analysis in the abstract, and everything to do with risk management as a discipline. Malpractice carriers, professional liability insurers, and corporate risk departments have spent decades building frameworks for managing exposure in fields where inconsistent professional judgment creates liability. Medical-legal consulting has, until recently, sat somewhat outside that framework — treated as a service relationship governed by reputation and referral rather than a risk category with its own credentialing standard.

That is changing, and it is changing for a straightforward reason: an unreliable medical-legal analysis is itself a source of risk, not merely a quality issue. A firm that builds a case theory on an analysis with an undisclosed methodological gap — a causation opinion formed before baseline was established, a standard-of-care judgment shaped by hindsight — is carrying exposure it may not have consciously accepted. That exposure surfaces at the worst possible time: after the theory has been built, the complaint filed, and the deposition scheduled around it.

Viewed through a risk-management lens, certification functions the same way any credentialing requirement functions in other high-stakes professional contexts: it converts an unmanaged, case-by-case risk into a managed, verifiable standard. A firm that requires or prefers Lexcura-certified analysts is doing the same thing a hospital does when it credentials physicians before granting privileges, or that a company does when it requires a licensed engineer to stamp a structural drawing — it is substituting a verifiable external standard for an internal, case-by-case judgment call that would otherwise have to be remade, imperfectly, every time.

This argument matters most for firms and litigation support departments operating at scale — handling enough medical-legal matters that methodology inconsistency, compounded across dozens or hundreds of cases a year, becomes a measurable rather than theoretical risk. For those firms, certification is not a matter of preference. It is the same category of decision as any other professional-standard requirement built into a risk-managed practice: a deliberate policy choice, made once, that reduces the number of case-by-case judgment calls the firm has to get right on its own.

PART FIVE

“

Competency should be demonstrated and tested at every stage, not assumed at the end of it.

THE LEXCURA CLINICAL INTELLIGENCE MODEL™

PART FIVE

WHAT THE PROGRAM ENTAILS

Inside the thirteen-module curriculum, from foundations to final examination.

Chapter 14 — Program Design Philosophy and the Standard Module

The Lexcura Clinical Intelligence Certification™ was built to a consistent internal standard across every module, so that a firm evaluating the credential can understand the rigor behind it without needing to review the coursework directly. Every module in the certification program is built around the same eight components, each serving a distinct purpose in moving a learner from introduction to demonstrated competency.

Each module opens with a module introduction that establishes the topic's objectives, explains why the topic matters to litigation specifically, and poses the core analytical question the module exists to answer. It continues with a structured slide-based teaching sequence — roughly fifteen to twenty slides per module — that builds the conceptual framework visually before extended narration, twenty to thirty minutes of detailed instruction per module, develops the concept fully, using real-world-style examples and explicit litigation application throughout.

Instruction alone is not treated as sufficient. Each module includes a workbook of guided exercises, reflection questions, and case-based analytical activities requiring the learner to apply the concept, not merely read about it. A knowledge check of five review questions reinforces the module's core concepts with immediate feedback, and a scored module quiz — ten to fifteen questions, mixing multiple-choice and scenario-based formats — tests application rather than recall. An answer key with full explanations closes the loop, and a module summary consolidates key takeaways before transitioning to the next pillar.

This structure repeats across all thirteen modules of the program, and that repetition is the point: the certification does not rely on any single module, or any single assessment, to validate competency. It builds a cumulative record of demonstrated understanding, module by module, before the program moves into applied case work in Modules 11 and 12, and comprehensive assessment in the Module 13 Final Certification Examination™ — each described further in the chapters that follow.

Chapter 15 — The Thirteen-Module Curriculum Path

The Certification Path

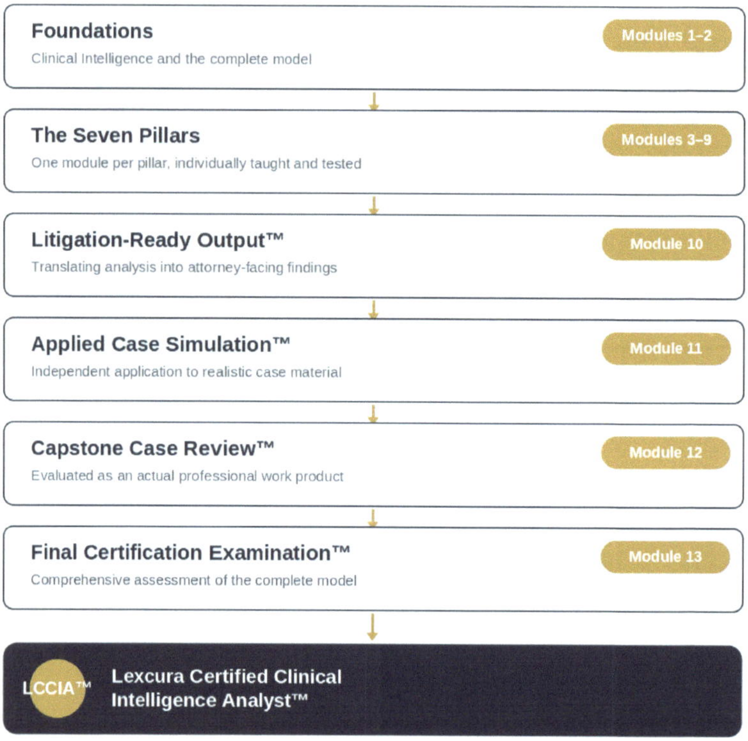

The certification curriculum moves learners through a deliberate progression: from foundational concepts, through each of the Seven Pillars individually, into applied practice, and finally into comprehensive assessment. What follows is an overview of that progression — the destination and purpose of each module, not its instructional content.

Module 1, Introduction to Clinical Intelligence™, establishes why traditional record review often fails to surface the findings that matter most, and introduces the foundational distinction between information and intelligence discussed in Chapter 2 of this guide.

Module 2, The Lexcura Clinical Intelligence Model™, introduces the complete framework and explains how the Seven Pillars function as a unified analytical system, establishing the methodology explored in the modules that follow.

Modules 3 through 9 correspond, one module each, to the Seven Pillars introduced in Part Two of this guide: Record Integrity™, Baseline Profiling™, Imaging Analysis™, Timeline Reconstruction™, Standard of Care Review™, Regulatory & Compliance Overlay™, and Causation Mapping™. Each module teaches the pillar's specific analytical question, the techniques used to answer it, and its place in the overall sequence.

Module 10, Litigation-Ready Output™, shifts from analysis to communication — teaching learners to translate completed clinical findings into a form that supports legal strategy and can be used directly by retaining attorneys.

Module 11, Applied Case Analysis and Case Simulation™, is the program's first fully integrated test: learners independently apply the complete methodology to realistic case material, moving from having learned the model to demonstrating they can use it.

Module 12, the Capstone Case Review™, raises the standard further. Rather than a training simulation, it is evaluated as an actual professional work product — the learner is expected to perform as though retained by an attorney, independently producing a complete Lexcura Clinical Intelligence Review™ across all Seven Pillars.

Module 13, the Final Certification Examination™, is described in full in the next chapter.

This structure means that, by the time a learner reaches certification, they have been taught each pillar individually, tested on each pillar individually, required to apply all seven pillars together on simulated case material, evaluated on an independent capstone work product, and comprehensively examined across the complete methodology. Certification is the outcome of that entire sequence, not any single stage of it.

Firms sometimes ask why the program devotes an entire module to communication — Module 10, Litigation-Ready Output™ — rather than treating it as a footnote to the analytical modules that precede it. The answer connects directly back to the trust problem described in Chapter 1: an analysis that is methodologically sound but poorly communicated still fails the attorney who has to use it. Teaching communication as its own disciplined module, positioned deliberately after all seven analytical pillars and before the applied case work in Modules 11 and 12, ensures that a certified analyst has practiced translating completed analysis into litigation-ready findings before ever being tested on doing so independently.

Chapter 16 — Applied Case Simulation and the Capstone Case Review™

Two stages of the certification program deserve particular attention from a referring firm, because they are where the credential moves from testing knowledge to testing performance.

Module 11's Applied Case Analysis and Case Simulation™ requires learners to apply the complete Lexcura Clinical Intelligence Model™ to realistic medical-legal case material independently, without the scaffolding of a single-pillar module. This is the point in the curriculum where the program stops asking "do you understand Record Integrity™" and starts asking "can you apply Record Integrity™, Baseline Profiling™, Imaging Analysis™, Timeline Reconstruction™, Standard of Care Review™, Regulatory & Compliance Overlay™, and Causation Mapping™, together, in the correct sequence, on a case you have not seen before."

Module 12's Capstone Case Review™ raises the bar again. It is explicitly not treated as a training exercise — it is evaluated as a professional work product, scored against a detailed rubric covering each pillar's contribution to the final analysis, from Record Integrity™ review through final causation findings. The learner is expected to function as though retained directly by an attorney, and the output is a complete Lexcura Case Review, produced independently and evaluated for the same qualities a retaining attorney would look for in real engagement: thoroughness, sequencing discipline, and litigation-ready clarity.

For a firm, these two stages are the practical answer to a reasonable skepticism about any credentialing program:

does this test actual capability, or just knowledge of terminology. The Applied Case Simulation and the Capstone Case Review™ exist specifically to ensure that certification reflects demonstrated, independently evaluated performance — not simply the ability to pass a multiple-choice quiz on definitions.

Chapter 17 — The Final Certification Examination™

The certification program concludes with Module 13, the Final Certification Examination™, a comprehensive assessment covering the complete Lexcura Clinical Intelligence Model™. Unlike the module-specific quizzes earlier in the curriculum, the final examination is organized around domains that span the entire methodology — foundational concepts, each of the Seven Pillars individually, integrated analysis across pillars, and case-based application — reflecting the same progression from foundational knowledge to integrated competency that runs through the whole program.

The examination is scored against a defined passing standard, and it is comprehensive by design: a candidate cannot pass by mastering some pillars while remaining weak in others, because the exam is explicitly structured to test the complete model rather than any single component of it. That is a deliberate design choice. A credential that could be earned while skipping mastery of, say, Baseline Profiling™ or Regulatory & Compliance Overlay™ would certify something less than full competency in the model, and full competency in the model is what the LCCIA™ designation is meant to represent.

This comprehensiveness is what allows a firm to rely on the credential without needing to ask which pillars a given analyst is strong or weak in. A partial credential would force a firm back into exactly the case-by-case evaluation the certification is designed to eliminate — asking, in effect, "which parts of the methodology can I actually trust this person to apply." A comprehensive final examination removes that question from the table entirely.

Successful completion of the Final Certification Examination™ — following the module curriculum, the applied case simulation, and the Capstone Case Review™ — is what confers the Lexcura Certified Clinical Intelligence Analyst™ designation. It is the final checkpoint in a program built, at every stage, around the same principle: competency should be demonstrated and tested, not assumed.

Chapter 18 — From Certification to Licensed Use™

Certification is the beginning of an analyst's relationship with the Lexcura Clinical Intelligence Model™, not the end of it. As discussed in Chapter 7, professional application of the methodology on live litigation matters — including governance, report production standards, attorney communication protocols, and operational implementation — is addressed through the separate Licensed Use Authorization™ Program.

For a referring firm, this pathway is worth understanding because it clarifies what to ask when structuring a consulting relationship. Certification confirms the analyst has mastered the methodology. Licensing addresses how that methodology is deployed in actual professional practice, under what governance standards, and with what operational safeguards. Firms building long-term relationships with Lexcura-trained analysts, or establishing internal vendor requirements, should treat these as two related but distinct questions — and should ask directly which pathway, or which combination, applies to a given analyst and a given engagement.

This structure is not incidental. It reflects the same discipline that runs through the entire model: separating distinct questions, addressing them in the correct order, and not allowing one form of validation to be mistaken for another.

PART SIX

“

An external standard the analyst did not design and cannot self-certify is a different category of assurance entirely.

THE LEXCURA CLINICAL INTELLIGENCE MODEL™

PART SIX

WORKING WITH CERTIFIED ANALYSTS

How to evaluate, engage, and build certification into firm standards.

Chapter 19 — Evaluating and Engaging a Certified Analyst

Understanding what the LCCIA™ credential certifies is only useful if it changes how a firm actually evaluates and engages analysts. A few practical practices follow directly from the material in this guide.

First, treat the credential as a floor, not a substitute for ordinary diligence. Certification confirms methodology; it does not confirm subject-matter fit for a particular case type, availability, communication style, or fee structure. A firm should still evaluate those factors independently, the same way it would for any consultant — the credential simply removes methodology from the list of open questions.

Second, ask which pathway applies. As discussed in Chapters 7 and 16, certification and licensure answer different questions. A firm structuring an engagement, particularly one involving report production intended for use in active litigation, should confirm directly whether the analyst's certification is paired with the professional authorization the engagement requires.

Third, use the structure of the methodology itself as a due-diligence tool. A firm that understands the Seven Pillars, even at the conceptual level presented in Part Two of this guide, can ask a certified analyst pointed, specific questions about how a given case was approached: How was record reliability assessed before the analysis began? What did the baseline profile establish? Was the timeline reconstructed independent of the causation conclusion? A certified analyst should be able to answer these questions specifically and confidently, because the methodology requires having answered them already, in sequence, as a condition of the analysis being complete.

Fourth, treat the credential as a communication tool with opposing counsel and the court, not only an internal quality standard. Being able to state that an analysis was performed by an analyst credentialed under a named, structured, externally administered methodology is itself useful information to have on the record — it is a specific, verifiable claim about process, not a general assertion of expertise.

Fifth, revisit the relationship periodically rather than treating certification as a one-time check. Certification confirms competency at the time it was earned; ongoing engagement with a certified analyst should still include the same relationship management a firm would apply to any trusted consultant — checking that the analyst continues to apply the methodology consistently across matters, and remaining alert to the same warning signs that would concern a firm about any professional relationship.

Chapter 20 — Building Certification into Firm Standards

Firms that repeatedly engage medical-legal analysts and consultants have an opportunity to move beyond case-by-case evaluation and build certification directly into their vendor and engagement standards. This is a natural evolution of the reputational and risk-management logic discussed in Chapter 11: rather than re-litigating an analyst's methodology on every new matter, a firm can establish, once, that Lexcura certification — or certification paired with the appropriate licensing, depending on the engagement — is a baseline requirement for medical-legal consulting relationships.

Doing so accomplishes several things at once. It gives litigation support directors a consistent, defensible basis for engagement decisions. It signals to referral partners and opposing counsel alike that the firm's medical-legal work product rests on a verifiable, structured standard rather than individual analyst reputation alone. And it creates a natural forcing function that rewards analysts who have invested in rigorous training — reinforcing exactly the kind of methodological consistency this guide has argued is now a practical necessity rather than a nice-to-have.

Firms considering this step do not need to treat it as an all-or-nothing policy. Many begin by preferring certified analysts where available, tracking outcomes and cross-examination experience across certified versus uncertified engagements, and tightening the standard as that internal evidence accumulates. What matters most is recognizing that this is a decision worth making deliberately, at the firm level, rather than leaving methodology entirely to the judgment of whichever partner happens to be staffing a given case.

Chapter 21 — The Analyst's Journey to Certification

A credential can feel abstract from the outside — a name on a report, a line on a resume. Describing what actually stands behind it matters here, because the rigor of the path is part of what makes the destination meaningful to a firm relying on it.

A candidate entering the Lexcura Clinical Intelligence Certification™ program begins with no assumed familiarity with the model. Module 1 starts from first principles — the distinction between information and intelligence discussed in Chapter 2 — before Module 2 introduces the complete Seven Pillar framework. From there, the candidate spends one module on each pillar in turn: Record Integrity™, Baseline Profiling™, Imaging Analysis™, Timeline Reconstruction™, Standard of Care Review™, Regulatory & Compliance Overlay™, and Causation Mapping™, each followed by guided workbook exercises, a knowledge check, and a scored quiz before the candidate is permitted to move forward.

This is a meaningfully slower and more demanding path than reading a manual or attending a seminar. By the time a candidate reaches Module 10 and begins learning to translate analysis into litigation-ready output, they have already been tested — repeatedly, in writing, against scored assessments — on their command of each individual pillar. Modules 11 and 12 then remove the scaffolding entirely: the Applied Case Analysis and Case Simulation™ requires the candidate to apply all seven pillars, independently, to case material they have not seen before, and the Capstone Case Review™ evaluates the result as an actual professional work product, not a practice exercise.

Only after clearing every one of those checkpoints does a candidate sit for the Module 13 Final Certification Examination™ — a comprehensive assessment spanning the entire methodology, which a candidate cannot pass by excelling in some pillars while neglecting others. The designation Lexcura Certified Clinical Intelligence Analyst™ is conferred only at the end of this complete sequence.

For a referring firm, the relevance of this description is practical rather than sentimental: it is a reminder that the credential does not represent a single test passed on a single afternoon. It represents a sustained demonstration of competency, built module by module, checked at every stage, and confirmed one final time against the complete model before the designation is awarded.

Chapter 22 — Frequently Asked Questions for Law Firms

Is this credential just another certificate, or does it actually test capability?

As described in Chapters 15 and 16, certification requires more than passing quizzes on individual pillars. It requires independently applying the complete methodology to case material in the Applied Case Simulation, producing an independently evaluated professional work product in the Capstone Case Review™, and passing a comprehensive final examination covering the entire model. A firm evaluating the credential should treat these integrated, applied assessments — not the module quizzes alone — as the strongest evidence that certification reflects real capability.

Does hiring a certified analyst guarantee a favorable outcome?

No credential can guarantee an outcome, and this guide has not argued otherwise. What certification provides is confidence in the process by which a conclusion was reached — confidence that record reliability was assessed before conclusions were drawn, that baseline was established before causation was evaluated, and that the standard of care was judged without the distortion of hindsight. A rigorous process narrows the range of ways an analysis can fail; it does not guarantee which way a close case will ultimately resolve.

How does certification relate to retaining someone as a testifying expert?

Certification speaks to methodology, not to a specific individual's qualification to testify as an expert witness in a given jurisdiction on a given medical specialty, which depends on separate considerations entirely outside the scope of this guide. What certification can offer in that context is a clear, structured account of how the underlying analysis was performed — often a meaningful asset when an expert's methodology is challenged on cross-examination or under a Daubert-type inquiry.

Should our firm require certification, or simply prefer it?

That is a firm-specific decision, and Chapters 11, 12, and 19 discuss both the reputational and risk-management considerations that inform it. Many firms begin by preferring certified analysts where available and tightening that preference into a requirement as they gain internal experience comparing outcomes across certified and uncertified engagements.

What is the difference between certification and the Licensed Use Authorization™ Program, again?

Certification confirms competency in the methodology. Licensing addresses professional application — governance, report production standards, and operational procedures for using the methodology on live matters. Chapters 8 and 18 address this distinction in full; the short version is that a firm structuring an engagement should confirm which pathway, or combination, applies to it.

Does this guide teach us the Lexcura Clinical Intelligence Model™ well enough that we don't need to engage a certified analyst?

No, and it is not intended to. This guide explains what each pillar is for and why the sequence matters, at the level a firm needs to evaluate the credential intelligently. It does not teach the analytical techniques, case-based judgment, or evaluative standards an analyst applies within each pillar — that instruction, along with the extensive testing that confirms it has been learned, is the content of the certification program itself.

Conclusion — The Case for Certification

The argument of this guide can be stated in a single sentence: medical-legal analysis performed without a consistent, tested methodology is a risk that is easy to carry quietly and expensive to discover late. The Lexcura Clinical Intelligence Certification™ exists to convert that risk into something a firm can verify in advance, rather than discover during a deposition.

The Lexcura Clinical Intelligence Model™ gives analysts a structured, seven-part sequence for turning medical documentation into litigation-ready findings — assessing record reliability first, establishing the patient's baseline before assessing causation, examining objective evidence directly, reconstructing an honest timeline, evaluating the standard of care without the distortion of hindsight, accounting for systemic and regulatory obligations, and only then mapping causation, before translating the completed analysis into attorney-facing work product. The certification program tests that methodology rigorously — through module-specific instruction and assessment, an applied case simulation, an independently evaluated Capstone Case Review™, and a comprehensive Final Certification Examination™ — before conferring the Lexcura Certified Clinical Intelligence Analyst™ designation.

For a law firm or referral partner, the practical upshot is straightforward. An LCCIA™-credentialed analyst represents a specific, verifiable claim: this person has been taught a defined methodology and has been tested, repeatedly and rigorously, on their ability to apply it — not merely to describe it. In a field where the alternative has long been trust extended on the basis of experience and reputation alone, that is a meaningfully different, and meaningfully more defensible, foundation to build a case on.

Appendix — Credential and Program at a Glance

Credential: Lexcura Certified Clinical Intelligence Analyst™ (LCCIA™)

Certifies: Demonstrated competency in the Lexcura Clinical Intelligence Model™ — instruction, module assessment, applied case simulation, Capstone Case Review™, and comprehensive final examination.

Does not certify: Authorization for professional application of the methodology on live litigation matters. That authorization is addressed separately through the Licensed Use Authorization™ Program.

The Seven Pillars, in sequence:

- Record Integrity™ — Can the record be trusted?
- Baseline Profiling™ — Who was the patient before the event?
- Imaging Analysis™ — Has the objective evidence been examined directly?
- Timeline Reconstruction™ — What happened, and when?
- Standard of Care Review™ — What should have happened?
- Regulatory & Compliance Overlay™ — What system duties applied?
- Causation Mapping™ — Did it actually change the outcome?

Program structure: Thirteen modules, each built around a consistent standard — module introduction, slide-based instruction, extended narration, guided workbook exercises, knowledge check, scored quiz, answer key, and module summary — followed by an applied case simulation

(Module 11), a fully evaluated Capstone Case Review™ (Module 12), and a comprehensive Final Certification Examination™ (Module 13) covering the complete methodology.

For firms: Certification should be treated as a verifiable baseline competency standard — a meaningful floor for evaluating and engaging medical-legal analysts, and a standard worth building directly into vendor and engagement requirements.

Glossary of Key Terms

Clinical Intelligence — The discipline of converting medical documentation into meaningful, litigation-relevant findings by organizing, connecting, and interpreting information rather than simply summarizing it. Distinguished throughout this guide from raw information, which documents events without explaining their significance.

Lexcura Clinical Intelligence Model™ — The proprietary, seven-part methodology developed by Lexcura Summit for medical-legal analysis, structured as the Seven Pillars applied in a fixed, interdependent sequence and translated into attorney-facing findings through Litigation-Ready Output™.

Record Integrity™ — The first pillar. Assesses whether a medical record is complete, internally consistent, and reliable enough to support the analysis that follows.

Baseline Profiling™ — The second pillar. Establishes a patient's pre-event condition, risk factors, vulnerabilities, and functional status, providing the context necessary for a fair causation analysis later in the sequence.

Imaging Analysis™ — The third pillar. Examines objective evidence — imaging studies, laboratory trends, continuous monitoring data — directly and on its own terms, rather than relying solely on narrative summaries or conclusions attached to that evidence.

Timeline Reconstruction™ — The fourth pillar. Organizes fragmented documentation into a coherent chronology capable of revealing delays, missed opportunities, and escalation failures.

Standard of Care Review™ — The fifth pillar. Compares the reconstructed timeline against the standard of care that reasonably applied at each decision point, using only what was knowable at the time rather than hindsight.

Regulatory & Compliance Overlay™ — The sixth pillar. Considers the policies, regulations, accreditation standards, and institutional obligations that governed the care setting, extending the analysis beyond individual provider conduct to systemic accountability.

Causation Mapping™ — The seventh and final analytical pillar. Determines whether the issues identified in the preceding six pillars actually changed the outcome, rather than merely coinciding with it.

Litigation-Ready Output™ — The discipline, taught in Module 10 of the certification curriculum, of translating a completed seven-pillar analysis into a form attorneys can immediately use — organized, prioritized, and framed to support legal strategy.

Lexcura Clinical Intelligence Certification™ — The structured educational program, described throughout Part Five of this guide, that teaches and tests competency in the Lexcura Clinical Intelligence Model™ across thirteen modules, an applied case simulation, a Capstone Case Review™, and a comprehensive final examination.

Lexcura Certified Clinical Intelligence Analyst™ (LCCIA™) — The credential awarded upon successful completion of the certification program, confirming demonstrated competency in the complete Lexcura Clinical Intelligence Model™.

Capstone Case Review™ — The Module 12 culminating assessment, evaluated as an actual professional work product rather than a training exercise, in which a candidate independently applies the complete methodology to produce a full Lexcura Case Review.

Licensed Use Authorization™ Program — The separate professional authorization pathway governing real-world application of the methodology, including governance, report production standards, and operational implementation, distinct from and administered after certification.

About the Author

Michelle Carroll is the Founder and Chief Executive Officer of Lexcura Summit and the originator of the Clinical Intelligence™ discipline.

Her work draws upon more than forty years of experience across healthcare and complex clinical review. Throughout her career, she became increasingly concerned by the gap between the amount of healthcare information available and the level of understanding that information often produced.

That concern led her to develop Clinical Intelligence as a disciplined method for reconstructing complex patient journeys, integrating evidence from multiple professional perspectives, and strengthening the quality of judgment upon which consequential healthcare and litigation decisions are made.

Michelle is the author of The Doctrine of Clinical Intelligence, the foundational text introducing the discipline, and developed the Lexcura Clinical Intelligence Certification™ described in this guide.

Through Lexcura Summit, she continues to advance the development, education, governance, and professional application of Clinical Intelligence.

About Lexcura Summit

Lexcura Summit developed the Lexcura Clinical Intelligence Model™ and administers the Lexcura Clinical Intelligence Certification™, the Licensed Use Authorization™ Program, and the Lexcura Certified Clinical Intelligence Analyst™ (LCCIA™) designation. Lexcura Summit's work centers on bringing a structured, consistent, and defensible methodology to medical-legal analysis — replacing variable, experience-based practice with a tested, repeatable standard that firms, referral partners, and the analysts themselves can rely on with confidence.

www.ingramcontent.com/pod-product-compliance
Lightning Source LLC
LaVergne TN
LVHW051136210926
848482LV00006B/329
9798997229764